Potty Training Multiples? Relax!

Tips to Guide You Through A Three-Day Potty
Training Process, Sanity Intact

By Victoria Adams

Cover design by Jacquelyn McGhee

ISBN 978-1482611342

First Edition

To my husband and children

Table of Contents

This book is based on opinion and personal experience. All information is intended for your general knowledge only and is not to be used as a substitute for medical advice or treatment.

Introduction

I am a mother of multiples. My triplets include two identical girls and one boy. Being a stay-at-home mother of triplets has been a dream come true, however my husband works a lot of hours to allow me to be able to stay at home with them. This often leaves me to handle the majority of the caregiving solo. Needless to say, I am always looking for the most efficient ways to accomplish everyday tasks. So when it came to potty training, I was looking for a stream-lined, structured process that wasn't going to put us through a ton of stress.

In my first book, *Triplets? Relax!*, I speak from the point of view of a mother who has navigated the first year of raising multiples. Trial and error helped me develop strategies and tricks of the trade that I share in a quick, easy to read reference. As a mother of multiples, I understand that my readers are busy and don't have time for a wordy book. Parents, especially parents of multiples, need a quick, to the point, easy to read manual that can give relevant information right when it's needed. With the success of my first book, and my subsequent success with potty training my triplets, I wanted to help my readers RELAX and let go of the fear associated with potty training.

Though the first two years comes with so many changes, I think potty training comes with a bad stigma that adds stress to the process. We see it as an insurmountable mountain that has to be climbed, all while we pull our hair out. To help parents of multiples get through this experience in one piece, I have focused on extracting the stress, breaking the process down, and making it simple.

I come from a family that potty trained around the two-year mark and, even though I had triplets, my family still expected my children to be trained around the time they turned two. Along with that, something inside of me was saying, "Potty train them earlier rather than later, before they gain too much control." Through extensive online research, discussions with friends and family members, I knew potty training my triplets around the time they turned two was the right thing to do.

I had heard all of the potty training horror stories and it always seemed as though the children in those stories were older. When I did the three-day potty training process, my kids had just turned two chronologically. However they were preemies. Although you do not need to adjust for age after two and a half, if you were adjusting for age, my children were between 22-23 months old. At this stage, I felt as though I had control and that I could make potty training just another habit I introduced without them realizing it. Another perk about training at this age is that toddlers have great excitement about anything new and tend to adapt to new routines quickly. Training them sooner rather than later is a major part of a smooth and successful potty training experience.

Chapter 1:

The Process Simplified – Day One

Tip 1:

The Three-Day Trick

I had heard of people potty training their kids over a few days. This was something that I had great interest in. I did some research online and decided that this was the approach I wanted to take. While online, I found that there were programs that I could purchase and soon found out that the potty training industry was full of unnecessary products that complicate a rather simple and natural process. I decided that, instead of purchasing products and programs, I would break down the potty training process to its simplest form. This book will guide you through that process and help you to introduce it into your already hectic life.

Tip 2:

Making the Connection

As the teacher, you have to mentally prepare yourself and not make potty training seem like such a monumental task. You need to understand that potty training, at its basic form, is to teach children the process of elimination. They are supposed to wet themselves all over the place at first until they make the connection. The second thing you must be prepared for is to be confined to one non-carpeted room in the house for two days (I chose our kitchen because of its linoleum flooring). Know that your two days of cleaning up messes is only going to be two days; after that, they will use the potty properly the <u>majority</u> of the time.

I say majority and not all of the time, because there are going to be accidents in the coming weeks and months. Like any major change and any process, it takes time. It can take up to six months for a child to completely be accident free. I can assure you that after the first two days, your children will understand the process. For the most part, my girls didn't have a lot of accidents after the first two days. My son took longer to become accident free. Still, he was going on the potty properly the majority of the day.

Tip 3:

What You Don't Need

- Pull-up diapers – It might be a surprise that this item is on the list, but the point of potty training is to get the child to recognize when they need to use the toilet, not another diaper. In most cases, they do not like the feeling of being soaking wet. Therefore, the feeling of becoming wet is an important learning tool for children. Pull-up diapers completely absorb liquid like regular diapers and do not allow a child to recognize when they are wet. Therefore, pull-up diapers eliminate a key learning tool.

- Training pants – Training pants work the same way as pull-up diapers, but with a different level of absorption. Even though they don't absorb the same amount of liquid as pull-up diapers, they are still absorbing too much liquid for the training process to be successful. Again, they eliminate an important indicator for children.

- A potty seat that has features such as a toilet paper holder, music, or anything designed to attract their attention – Children should focus on the process and the potty's specific function; it's not a toy. The most important feature of a potty seat is the design, and in Tip 5 in this chapter I go into further detail of the exact type of potty you will need.

Tip 4:

What You Do Need

- A potty seat for each child – In the beginning, the kids like to have their own potty seat, but there will also be many times when they will all sit on the potty and go to the bathroom at the same time. You don't want them to have to wait.

- Underwear – regular, non-absorbent underwear. The kids love picking out their favorite character or design to wear.

- The travel potty – This is so important that I dedicate Tip 2 in chapter 5 to addressing it.

- A potty seat that sits on top of your adult toilet seat for when you start teaching them to use the big toilet.

- A non-carpeted room – For the first couple of days, your children are supposed to get wet all over the place! That is how they learn. Confining yourself to a non-carpeted room makes clean-up a breeze.

- Easy to clean toys for entertainment while in the training room. Once the excitement of being in a different room wears down, they will need something to do. If your play area is already non-carpeted, make sure to remove any stuffed animals, books, or toys that would be hard to clean. Keep only the items that can easily be wiped down.

- Lots of liquid – I let them drink milk or water all day long to fill their bladders.

- Warm weather is ideal for potty training because the kids won't be fully dressed. This also allows you the option to go outside.

Tip 5:

The Perfect Potty

I tried five potty seats total. All had different designs that ranged from a number of features (and price ranges) to very basic. I had a potty with wipes and toilet paper holders that could later be used as a stool, a potty with a padded seat that could transfer onto an adult toilet, a potty with a one-piece design, and one that sat on top of the adult toilet. I was surprised by how many designs there were and how they all still seemed to create a mess. The urine would be channeled down and around into compartments, down the side, or sometimes through gaps in the seat. The seats that turned into stools had plastic grids that would get urine in all the corners and were a pain to clean.

Then I found the most well-designed potty and it was only $9.88! The **Summer Infant Stackable Potty**, which I purchased from Walmart.com (let me state that I am not connected with or getting compensation from the companies that I list in this book). The Summer Infant Stackable Potty was the only potty seat that didn't create a mess. This potty chair is a must have for both boys and girls, but even more so for boys, as they have a hard time urinating straight down. This potty seat has a nice, large splash guard and is big and sturdy enough for boys. The other potty seats I bought seemed unable to hold my son's heavier weight well, and/or would come apart when he sat on them. The Summer Infant Stackable Potty is big and sturdy and has a large back to lean on safely. It is also easy to clean. There are similar designs out there, but as long as you get a potty that replicates this design you should have no issues.

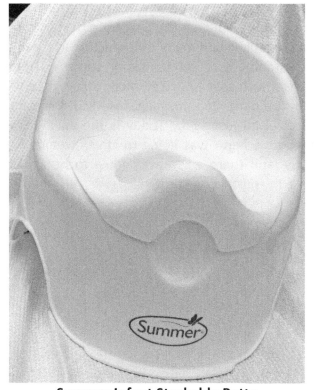

Summer Infant Stackable Potty

Tip 6:

Just Do It

I was contemplating the best time to start the training. I looked at scheduling and many other factors to try to create the perfect environment to set us up for success. I found myself analyzing so much that I created more stress than if I had just started the training. One morning, I walked down the stairs to start the day and just said, "Today is the day." I was tired of thinking about when I was going to start. I realized that every day is busy, and there was never going to be a perfect time. Don't make my mistake. Just do it!

Tip 7:

To Split Them Up or Not?

Because I have triplets that include both genders, I decided to start with the girls first and train my son once the girls got the hang of it. As most boys can be, my son was a bit behind my girls developmentally. I figured he'd benefit from the extra time. Depending on your set of multiples, you may want to train them all together or split them apart. A set of boy/girl twins might be easy to train together, as would higher order multiples of the same gender.

Tip 8:

Set Up

I went into the kitchen and childproofed the entire area with gates, oven knob covers, cabinet locks, etc. We were going to spend two days in there and the kids would be running around, so it needed to be safe. I set up a potty in the kitchen for each child and had them wear only underwear. I kept lots of extra clean underwear near me. During day one, they will be going through them fast. You will also need something to clean the messes, such as paper towels and wipes.

Tip 9:

Day One – Can I Have a Raincoat?

Day one is the messiest. Remember, children have been trained to walk around with diapers on and just go to the bathroom without thinking, so this process can be a shock to them. Children need a number of accidents to realize what is going on and start to make the connection and learn from it. I brought the two girls into the kitchen and had my son in a separate room that was adjacent to us so I could keep an eye on him. The three-day method requires an incredible amount of focus on your part. Catching your toddlers in the act of going to the bathroom and showing them what they should be doing is the priority. The training started with the girls going to the bathroom as they were standing up. I would immediately pick them up and put them on the potty. I watched them like a hawk to see the first sign of them going to the bathroom so I could get them on the potty. This is the first step to make the connection between the feeling of having to go to the bathroom and making it to the potty seat. For bowel functions, I followed the same process of having them sit on the potty immediately. They usually provided more of a warning when a bowel movement was coming. They usually acted worried or nervous because they weren't sure what to do and this is when you need to guide them to sit on the potty.

Show excitement and give praise every time they use the potty seat. Also, make sure to give each bathroom function a name. Since my kids knew what water was, I started by describing it as "yellow water". It was easy for them to understand that they could make yellow water. Use terms that you are comfortable with for urine and bowel functions and they will start learning and talking about what is going on.

Tip 10:

Day One – Good-Bye, Daytime Diapers!

From the start of potty training, my kids no longer wore diapers during the day. In fact, I changed the name of diapers to naptime diapers (you can come up with your own) because they were only for wearing when sleeping. Changing the name helped them understand that underwear was for the day and diapers were for sleeping.

Hint: For the naptime diaper, I tried pull-up diapers and found that they didn't give as snug of a fit as regular diapers. There was no way to tighten them and they seemed especially loose around the leg area. Because of this, they would leak while the children were sleeping, so I stuck with regular diapers at night since they gave a snug fit and didn't leak.

Tip 11:

Day One – Keeping to Your Schedule

After a whirlwind of a morning, it was time for the kids to nap. After hours of practice and putting the girls on the potty, they still seemed clueless. I went on with the rest of my daily routine, which included a nap first and then lunch. I would shortly see the importance of taking a break and going back to the normal schedule for a few hours.

Tip 12:

Day One – Refreshed and Ready

After the kids napped, I had them sit on the potty. Going to the bathroom as soon as they wake up will become a big part of your new routine. I put underwear back on them to eat lunch. What was interesting was that the breaks consisting of a nap and lunch seemed to refresh them. After lunch they started to show that they were making a connection between the potty seat and going to the bathroom. It is a lot to learn. They have to learn to pull down their underwear, sit down, and then go to the bathroom. For them, there was never any order to it before. But I was quite impressed when I would see them at least attempting to make it to the potty, trying to get their underwear down, or even just sitting on the potty. Now that there was a connection made, it was time to add a magical element.

Tip 13:

Day One – Incentives

During our normal days, my kids had a designated play area in the house. They were not free to roam anywhere outside their play area. However, they soon learned that potty training came with privileges. Once they were making a connection between eliminating and sitting on the potty, it was time to reward them. I first started by taking them to the bathroom and letting them flush the toilet. This was exciting because they got to go to an area outside of their play zone, they got to flush the toilet, and they got to do it one-on-one with mommy (a rare and special opportunity for a multiple). After doing that a few times, I added the next element that was truly magical; a treat! I am very conscious of what they eat, so at first I thought giving them blueberries would be enough of a treat. I soon found out that although they loved blueberries, they didn't give the <u>wow</u> factor. That is when I decided to give them a few wheat pieces from a box of Lucky Charms cereal. They gave that wow factor because they had some sugar on them. I was comfortable using food as a reward since it would only be for a short amount of time. You can use anything you are comfortable with, but a treat goes a long way. In fact, treats were the turning point for one of my daughters. She soon realized that she could work the system, and I let her do it!

Tip 14:

Day One – Songs and Books

Although it is not necessary, I did find the kids to be very engaged in the Elmo Potty Song (you can Google it and play it on your computer). They really took to the song and watched Elmo go through the potty process. The song addresses the whole process in a cute way. I also had some children's books about going potty. Both reinforced excitement for the potty, making the day all about the potty and making it fun!

Tip 15:

Day One – Finishing Up

As you get the kids ready for bed and put their newly named naptime diapers on, think of all that you have accomplished! You have laid the foundation for success for the next day and the other days to come.

Chapter 2:

The Process Simplified – Day Two

Tip 1:

Day Two – Today is Easier

My kids were excited to see that we would be spending another day in the kitchen. After all, it was still a new environment and they were going to get to do all these new things like the day before. The morning is a refresher course to remind them that they need to sit on the potty when they have to go to the bathroom. It is an exciting reminder that they get treats and get to flush the toilet. I remember wondering what my water bill was going to be from flushing the toilet so much.

During day two, my one daughter learned that the more often she urinated, the more often she got Lucky Charms. From that day forward, the amount of accidents she had can literally be counted on one hand. She took to potty training immediately because of the incentives, and I couldn't believe how fast that happened. However, every child is different, even with multiples. For my other daughter and son, it was a different story.

Tip 2:

Day Two – Letting Them Take Over

On day two, I no longer watched them like a hawk. I didn't want them to depend on me to let them know when to go potty. Now they had to learn to recognize the signs without my assistance. I didn't completely leave them on their own, I just wasn't as attentive in order to give them a chance to recognize the need to go potty and act on their own. Day two was not accident free, but it was a world of difference from the previous day.

Tip 3:

Day Two – Winding Down

You will probably be tired of being confined to one room, but the worst is over. Your kids should now have the process down in the room that you have been using. It is now time to expose them to the next obstacle: distraction. You will find that they thrive in the room you have been in for two days because using the potty seat is their main focus. It is now time to transfer their new knowledge to their regular environment. Ours was a carpeted living room. I decided to let them in their area for an hour or so at the end of day two to start the transition and help prep them for the next day.

Chapter 3:

The Next Phase

Tip 1:

Day Three – Back to Normalcy

Day three had setbacks. The kids were in a different environment and their potty seats were in a new location in their playroom. Now that they were back in their regular environment, there were distractions, and they were no longer focused on just going to the bathroom. They were also engaged in playing with the toys they had been away from for two days.

Now that the potty process is not the main focus they will forget from time to time and accidents will occur. Anything that looks like a setback can be frustrating, but try to keep in mind how much progress has been made in such a short time. Look at the ratio of times your children have used the potty seat to the number of accidents. The potty seat usage will outnumber the accidents.

The most important thing for long term success is to stick with it! Don't think it will be easier or more convenient for you to put a diaper back on. As I said before, I <u>never</u> went back to letting them wear diapers during the day. To avoid getting the carpet soaking wet from an accident, I put sweatpants on them. It still let them feel that they were wet, and the pants absorbed most of the liquid. As a reminder, take out any stuffed animals or anything that might not be easy to clean. Accidents happen, and you want them to happen on easy to clean surfaces.

Tip 2:

Day Three – Adding Incentives

Day three brings on more changes, but also more incentives. I started a sticker chart, which can be found on the next two pages. I allowed an additional reward for pooping on the potty. The kids got two treats (usually a strawberry and Lucky Charms) and they got to sit in the grown-up area while they ate their treats. The incentives of stickers, food, and freedom were what really made the kids buy into the system. With multiples, there is always constant reinforcement of the system because someone is going potty or getting praise or a reward. If one child gets a treat for going potty, it's a reminder to the other children what they can do to achieve a reward, too.

Note: There is a two-sided potty chart on the next page that you can tear out to use. You can also go the Web site listed under the chart to print a larger version.

_____ Potty Chart

Image provided by
The Scrap Shoppe http://thescrapshoppeblog.com

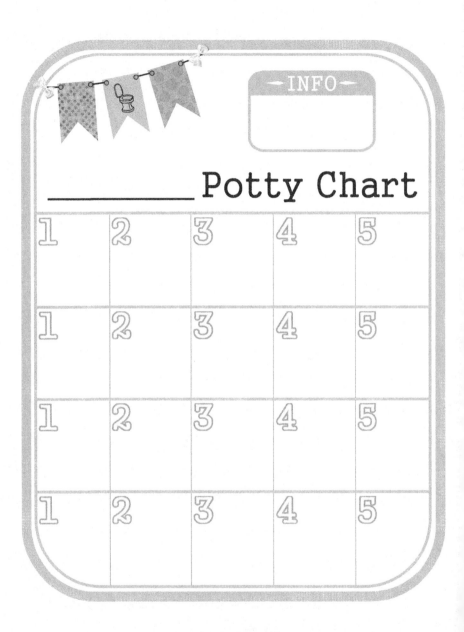

INFO

_____ Potty Chart

1	2	3	4	5
1	2	3	4	5
1	2	3	4	5
1	2	3	4	5

Image provided by
The Scrap Shoppe http://thescrapshoppeblog.com

Tip 3:

Beach Towel

I took a large beach towel and put it under the potties. I found that sometimes (especially with boys) they miss the potty. The towel would prevent the carpet from getting wet, and then I could just throw the towel into the wash.

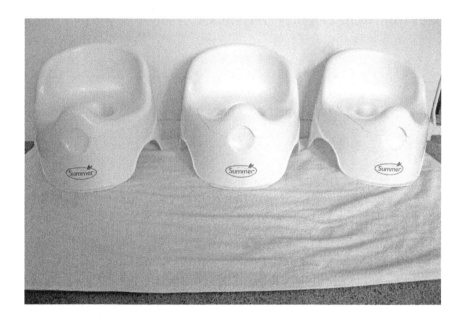

Tip 4:

The Onesie Dilemma

With triplets, I had a large supply of onesies, but during potty training, onesies do not work well. The kids didn't know how to unsnap them, or the tail of the onesie would dip into the potty seat. I had so many onesies; I did not want to stop using them and have to buy t-shirts, so I came up with some solutions. The first was to tuck the tail in the back of the onesie neck. This worked for a while, but sometimes the tail fell out and got wet. I then realized I could bring the tail around the side and snap it in the front using one snap. This worked great for a while.

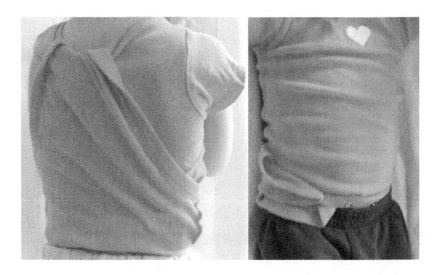

Pictures of the onesie tucked in back and snapped around the side.

Once I had the time to sit down, I cut the tail off and sewed a stich across the back. If you don't own a sewing machine or don't know someone who could stitch the back, cutting off the tail without a stitch may give you longer use of the onesies.

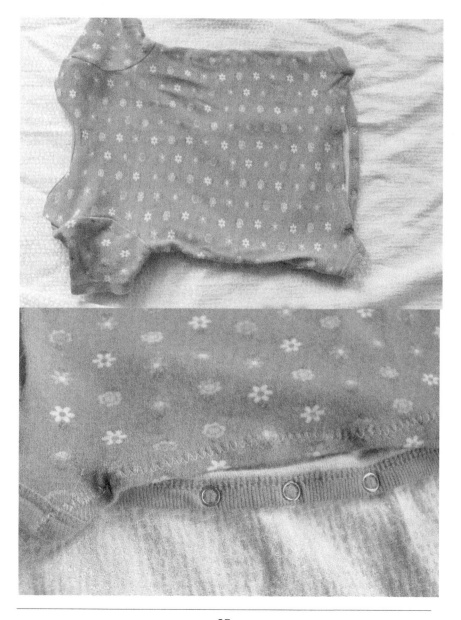

Tip 5:

Hands Off

You may be wondering how to get your kids to stop playing with the potty seats when they are not in use. Kids are curious and my three went straight to work disassembling and studying the potties. I made it clear in the beginning that they do not touch or play with the potties. It took a few days for the novelty to wear off. Make it really clear that you are not happy when they touch the potty seats and that it is unacceptable unless they are going to the bathroom. If you have a discipline system in place like corner time, then you may want to implement it after the first few days.

Tip 6:

Toilet Avoidance

As I mentioned in Chapter 2, Tip 1, one of my daughters took to the process by day two and one did not. The daughter who took longer to potty train was urinating on the potty but had issues with pooping on the potty. She would cry, refuse to sit on the toilet, and end up going in her underwear. To fix the issue, I had her run around with no bottoms on, and it worked. When she was wearing underwear, it still provided some sense of security to poop in, but with that layer gone, she didn't feel like she had anything secure to go to the bathroom in. For a secure feeling, she turned to the potty seat and started pooping on it without issue. I let her run around bottomless for a few days. I then tried her with underwear again. By that time, she was in the habit and comfortable with going poop on the potty.

Tip 7:

The Adult Toilet

At some point in the first week or two, it is a good idea to introduce them to the adult toilet with a different potty seat that fits on top of the adult toilet seat (see picture).

Once they had the system down on their training potties, I would have them go on the adult potty first thing in the morning. They got comfortable with using a different potty seat and with the functions of the bathroom. The rest of the day they would use their training potty that I had set up in their play area.

Chapter 4:

Looking Like Pros

Tip 1:

Time to Wean Off of Incentives

I went through the process of incentives and praise for about two weeks. I felt like all I did during the day was walk back and forth from their play area to the bathroom cleaning potties. It felt like more work than when they were all wearing diapers! The kids were going as often as they could because they wanted their incentives. The system was working, the kids were doing everything right, but it was becoming a lot of extra work because the incentives motivated the kids to go as much as they could. It was time to wean them off of incentives and make going to the potty a regular daily habit.

The first step to weaning them off incentives is to make them choose one incentive. Now they no longer got to do the sticker chart, flush the toilet, and get a few Lucky Charms. They had to pick one. After they adjusted to having just one incentive, I took down the sticker chart and removed the privilege to flush the toilet. I only had the Lucky Charms incentive. I would no longer give them Lucky Charms unless they asked. When they asked, I would sometimes ignore the request. Again, like every stage you have been through with the kids, they adapt. They soon would ask and forget, or just not ask at all. Once the incentives are out of the picture, you will start to see the time between using the potty increase. They are no longer going to the bathroom to get an incentive. They are now simply going to the bathroom when they have to.

Tip 2:

Weaning Off of Diapers When Sleeping

This is one area I didn't worry about. They were young and I figured this process would happen naturally. The girls would wet their diapers at night, and then after about one month they started having dry diapers upon waking. After three days of dry diapers, I stopped putting them on. They haven't worn diapers at night since. One of my girls was faster at getting rid of diapers than the other, but I was still impressed with their progress. My son took much longer to stop wetting diapers at night.

Chapter 5:

Going Out

Tip 1:

The Next Phase – Getting Out of the House

After two weeks of staying at home or playing in the backyard and keeping the potty close by, I decided it was time to go out in public without diapers. I was scared. I was not sure what to expect. However, it was the right time to make the transition, and trips out of the house were uneventful. Do what you feel comfortable with and what you can manage, but don't wait too long to start getting out of the house. Because I did it early on in the process, they were fine with going on different toilets in different locations.

Tip 2:

What to Bring

In the beginning, I brought the whole diaper bag on trips outside the house. Slowly I realized I was never going into the diaper bag and was able to downsize to a much smaller bag. However, there was one piece of equipment that I consider a must have. It is called the Kalencom 2-in-1 Potette® Plus. When I first started taking the kids out in public with no diapers on, I was carrying around a potty seat for them to go in the car. Then I purchased the Potette® Plus for only $16.00! It can be purchased at www.kalencom.com. This potty seat folds in for easy carrying (it fit in my diaper bag or my purse). It folds out into a standing seat for a child to use in the car or anywhere! Another great feature (and make sure you buy the Potette® PLUS, because there is one out there that does not have this feature) is that the legs can lock flat out to line up with the seat so that it can go on top of an adult toilet seat.

Hint: The Potette® Plus has liners that are sold separately. The child's waste goes into this bag and then you can take the bag, tie it, and throw it away. It is super clean! However, instead of purchasing these special bags, I have found that regular grocery bags fit this model and I would throw something absorbent inside like a diaper doubler or even a paper towel.

The Kalencom 2-in-1 Potette® Plus **folded to fit in a diaper bag or purse.**

The Kalencom 2-in-1 Potette® Plus **in standing position to be used anywhere.**

The Kalencom 2-in-1 Potette® Plus **lays flat to fit on top of an adult toilet.**

Tip 3:

Car Seat Protection

No parent wants to have to disassemble the car seat for potty accidents. I came up with a great way to protect the car seat when they were still early in their training. I found that regular diapers fit nicely in car seats because they have cut outs for the side seatbelts. I would place a diaper in the car seat and use it like a liner. I would then put the kids in the car seat in their underwear. This gave me some relief that if they did have an accident in the car, the car seat was protected.

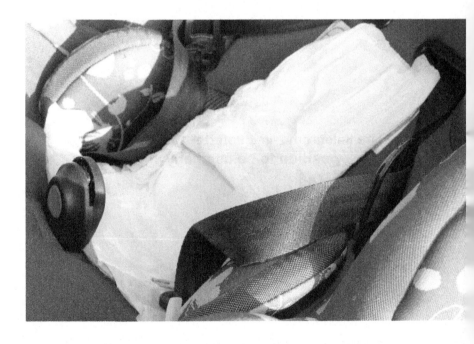

Tip 4:

Bathroom on Wheels

In Tip 2 of this chapter, I mentioned being able to have the space for a potty seat to be set up in the vehicle. I have a minivan, which gives enough space on the floor behind the passenger seat for this set up. If you don't have a minivan, try to find and clear out a space for a potty to be placed. It is super convenient to have this option. It serves as your personal bathroom on wheels. I could have them all go to the bathroom before or after we went to a store. It was also a great back-up restroom. If I found that the restroom in a store was not as clean as I would like, I would have them go in the minivan.

Chapter 6:

Special Tips for Potty Training Boys

Tip 1:

Pros and Cons to Splitting Them Up

Once my two girls had the hang of potty training, it was time to train my son. There were pros and cons to splitting them up. The pros were that my son now had a great understanding of the potty process because he had watched his sisters, seen the incentives, and become very interested. He was even excited to wear underwear. It gave him some additional time to catch up to where the girls were developmentally. The cons were that I had to start the process all over again, beginning with the two-day confinement in the kitchen.

Tip 2:

Extra Steps

I soon realized that boys need a few extra steps in the potty training process. Girls can sit on a potty seat and urinate straight down into the container. Boys sit on a potty seat and urinate straight out at you! I had to teach my son to tuck down and close his legs. Tucking would assure that he would urinate directly into the container, and closing his legs would keep the tuck in place. This is also why the potty seat you choose will make or break you. You will need a potty seat with a very large splash guard. Most potty seats do not have large enough splash guards, including the potty seats that go on the adult toilets. On the potty seats for the adult toilets, they can urinate over the guard and even in between the space that is created by the potty seat and the adult toilet. Keep your eye out for this so you know what to look for and don't get sprayed. Because of this, it is a must to teach these extra steps.

Tip 3:

Toddler Boxers

Boys' underwear has a very thick band around the waist. This makes them very hard for a toddler to pull up or down by themselves or get them on straight. I ended up switching to toddler boxers. There aren't a lot of companies that make boxers at such a small size. I was only able to find two options at www.amazon.com. The boxers have a much looser waist band and are easier for a toddler to get on and off. I found that boxers helped my son achieve the process of pulling down his boxers and sitting on the potty in a timely manner without having to struggle with a thick elastic band.

Tip 4:

The Reminder

I went through the two-day training with my son and he did a nice job initially. After the first two days of potty training, my son would use the potty the majority of the time, but he did have more accidents than the girls once it was day three and he was back in our regular environment. Walking around in wet or soiled underwear and pants did not bother him as much as it did the girls. I talked to other mothers and the advice was the same: "Give him time" and "Boys just take longer". I found that I needed to remind my son every two hours or so to go to the potty to avoid accidents. I knew he understood the process since he was accomplishing it successfully most of the day, but there was an element of disinterest on his part. I still never went back to diapers during the day and, over time, he really did become accident free. You may just find it to be a much longer process for boys than girls.

Tip 5:

Learning the Difference Between Boys and Girls

If you have both genders in the house that are potty training at the same time, they are going to learn that there is a difference between boys and girls. The girls noticed that my son had extra instructions about tucking, so I had to explain that he was a boy and he was different. They also see each other going to the bathroom and are curious why they look different from each other, so I explained the difference. If you have both genders in the house potty training at the same time, prepare yourself with an answer for this topic. It can be as simple as boy pee-pee versus girl pee-pee. You can explain it in whichever way you are most comfortable.

In Conclusion

I hope that this book provided you with some valuable ideas that you can implement or use to complement your potty training process. Potty training is a major milestone, but it can be broken down into simple parts to show that it is just a natural process and doesn't have to be the dreaded challenge that it is sometimes made out to be. In the first two years, there are so many milestones that our kids go through. It seems that, with each step, we are also inundated with products to try to make the process easier. It can be overwhelming. That is why breaking these tasks down to their simplest form is sometimes best. It is turning a mountain into a molehill. For your convenience here are the products and resources that were mentioned in this book.

- Summer Infant Stackable Potty – Type into any search engine for purchasing options.
- Kalencom 2-in-1 Potette® Plus – www.kalencom.com
- Elmo Potty Song – Type into any search engine to find the video.
- Free printable sticker chart – The Scrap Shoppe – http://thescrapshoppeblog.com
- Toddler boxers – www.amazon.com – Type in "toddler boxers". There are two options in size 2T/3T from the companies Fruit of the Loom and Hanes.

As a parent of multiples, you are aware of the attention your kids get when you are out in public. Being a mother of triplets, I always get stopped when we are out. Once people found out that they are potty trained and only two years old, I usually get a pat on the back. It is a great feeling and something to be very proud of. I often think about how different it would be if they were still in diapers and how much they seem to have grown since being potty trained. It is now just a part of our daily life. Don't psych yourself out by thinking this is a daunting process. Psych yourself up for the leaps and bounds you are about to make in such a short amount of time! And when the going gets tough, take a deep breath and remind yourself to stay cool and *relax*!

Made in United States
North Haven, CT
15 April 2023

35478532R00046